JAN 2010

ROBOZONES

ROBOT BRAINS

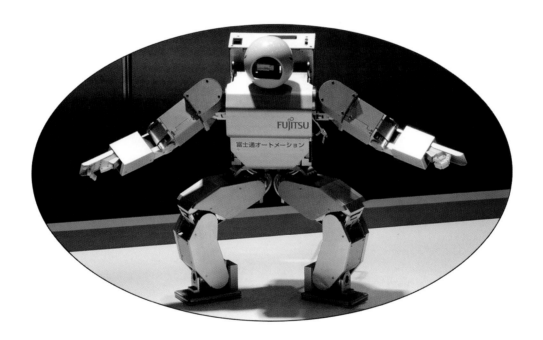

DAVID JEFFERIS

Crabtree Publishing Company

www.crabtreebooks.com

INTRODUCTION

A robot is a machine that is controlled by a computer program to perform work by itself. A robot may also be commanded by a person using a control box that is linked to the robot by cable or radio.

A robot's brain is its central computer. It processes information and runs the robot's mechanical systems.

Researchers are trying to develop robots with **artificial intelligence** (A.I.), or the ability to "think" and "learn" like humans.

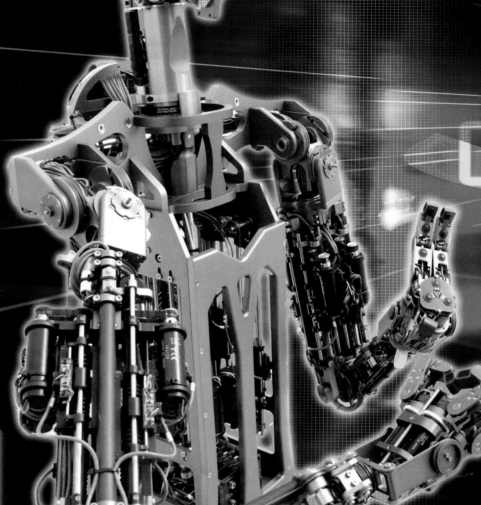

Crabtree Publishing Company
www.crabtreebooks.com

PMB 16A
350 Fifth Ave.
Ste. 3308
New York

616 Welland Ave
St. Catharines, ON
Canada
L2M 5V6

Edited by
Isabella McIntyre

Coordinating editor
Ellen Rodger

Editors
Rachel Eagen
L. Michelle Nielsen

Production coordinator
Rose Gowsell

Educational advisor
Julie Stapleton

Technical consultant
Mat Irvine FBIS

Created and produced by
David Jefferis/Buzz Books

©2007 David Jefferis/Buzz Books

**Library and Archives Canada
Cataloguing in Publication**

Jefferis, David
    Robot brains / David Jefferis.
(Robozones)
Includes index.
ISBN-13: 978-0-7787-2886-3 (bound)
ISBN-10: 0-7787-2886-2 (bound)
ISBN-13: 978-0-7787-2900-6 (pbk)
ISBN-10: 0-7787-2900-1 (pbk)

    1. Robots--Juvenile literature. 2.
Robotics--Juvenile literature.
I. Title. II. Series.
TJ211.2.J43 2006
j629.8'92   C2006-902860-5

**Library of Congress
Cataloging-in-Publication Data**

Jefferis, David.
    Robot brains / written by David Jefferis.
        p. cm. -- (Robozones)
    Includes index.
    ISBN-13: 978-0-7787-2886-3 (rlb)
    ISBN-10: 0-7787-2886-2 (rlb)
    ISBN-13: 978-0-7787-2900-6 (pbk)
    ISBN-10: 0-7787-2900-1 (pbk)
    1. Robots--Juvenile literature. 2.
Robotics--Juvenile literature. I.
Title. II. Series: Jefferis, David.
Robozones.
    TJ211.2.J45 2006
    629.8'9263--dc22
                     2006016040

Pictures on these pages, clockwise from above
left:
1   Part of a computer circuit.
2   A domo robot handles objects, learning
about their size and shape.
3   Honda Asimo robot.
4   Fujitsu HOAP-1 robot.

Previous page shows:
Fujitsu HOAP-2 robot.

CONTENTS

EARLY ROBOTICS

Robotics is the study of robots. People have been interested in robotics for thousands of years. The latest trends in robotics help people in their daily lives at work and at home.

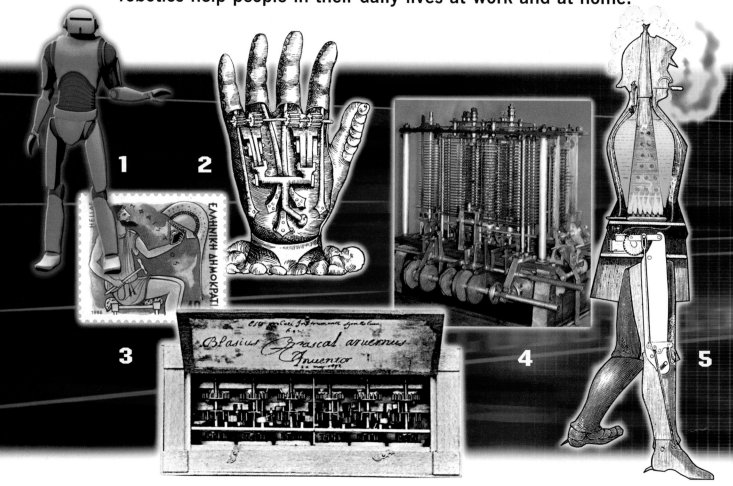

1 2 3 4 5

▲ Many steps were involved in the development of robots.
1 Talos, and a stamp showing its maker, the god Hephaestus.
2 The design for an artificial hand, drawn about 1530 A.D.
3 This mechanical calculator was built in 1642.
4 The Difference Engine, a type of early computer made in 1823.
5 George Moore's steam man of 1893 had a gas boiler and water supply in its chest.

People have been dreaming of robots for thousands of years. The very first robot stories were told about 4,500 years ago in ancient Greece. According to myth, the god Hephaestus created a metal man called Talos to guard the island of Crete. Talos was a strong robot that glowed red hot and crushed its victims with its powerful arms.

In the 1500s, craftspeople made artificial limbs for soldiers who had lost arms or legs in battle. Hands with working parts are distant ancestors of the computer-controlled grippers used in today's robots. In 1893, American inventor George Moore built a metal man that could walk. The machine was powered by a **steam engine** with the steam escaping through an **exhaust pipe** disguised as a cigar!

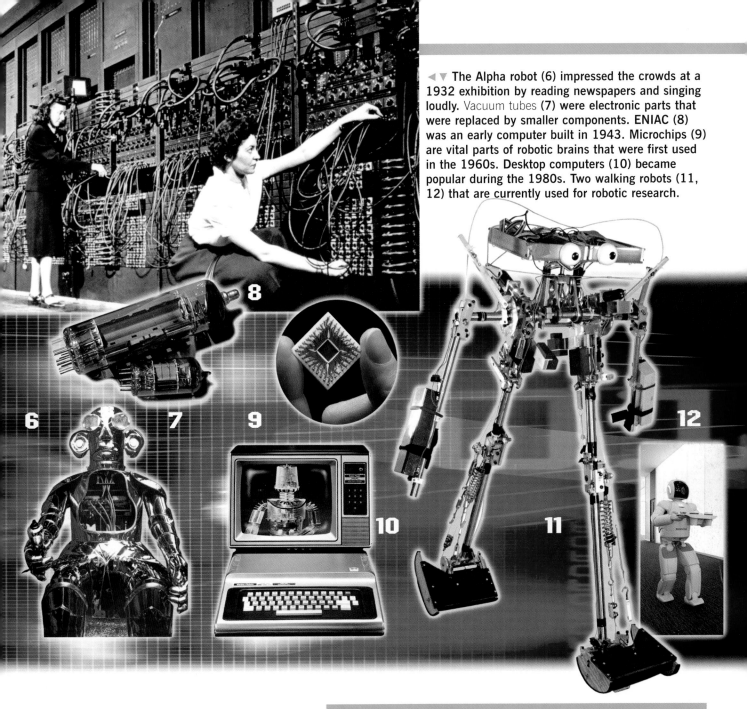

The Alpha robot (6) impressed the crowds at a 1932 exhibition by reading newspapers and singing loudly. Vacuum tubes (7) were electronic parts that were replaced by smaller components. ENIAC (8) was an early computer built in 1943. Microchips (9) are vital parts of robotic brains that were first used in the 1960s. Desktop computers (10) became popular during the 1980s. Two walking robots (11, 12) that are currently used for robotic research.

These early robotic inventions looked impressive, but none had a controlling brain. This had to wait until the invention of the computer.

The ENIAC (Electronic Numerical Integrator And Computer) was an important early computer. Made at the University of Pennsylvania in 1946, it was the first large-scale **digital** computer that could tackle a variety of computing problems. Computers now operate on similar principles.

ROBOFACTS: THE TURING TEST

Alan Turing was a British mathematician who worked on computers in the 1950s. Turing suggested that one day computers might be able to think. The term for a thinking computer is artificial intelligence (A.I.). Turing's test determines if such a machine really is intelligent.

The test consists of a typed-out conversation between a human and two hidden "people" - another human and an A.I. computer. Answers to the questions are then evaluated. A computer that generates human-like answers is said to have artificial intelligence. So far, no computer has come close to sounding intelligent.

Alan Turing is featured on this special stamp

BRAIN-CHIP

Robots are controlled by tiny computer parts called microchips. **They process information at lightning speed.**

▲ The "legs" of a microchip are connectors that link it to other parts.

The microchip, or simply "chip," is made of thousands of parts, such as **transistors**, in a tiny electronic **circuit** about the size of a fingernail. Parts are laid out in very thin layers on a slice, or chip, of **silicon**. It is these tiny calculating parts that are the brains of any computing device, including all robots. It takes only one microchip to operate a pocket calculator or a simple robotic toy. Complex machines, such as personal computers or robots that weld things together, may use dozens or even hundreds of chips.

▲ The Hitachi Company's Emiew robots were built to advance robotic communication abilities. An Emiew has a vocabulary of about 100 words.

Microchips are ideal for controlling robots because they are small and can process information very quickly. The smaller the computer, the shorter the distances signals need to travel inside it. This makes calculations quicker for smaller computers. Fewer parts are also important because there is less to go wrong.

▶ Robots come in all shapes and sizes, although few look close to the human-like robots of science fiction. This welding robot is bolted to the floor and has only one arm.

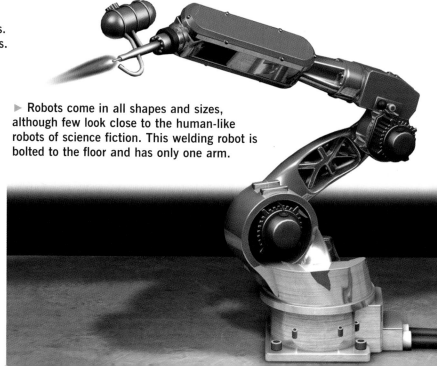

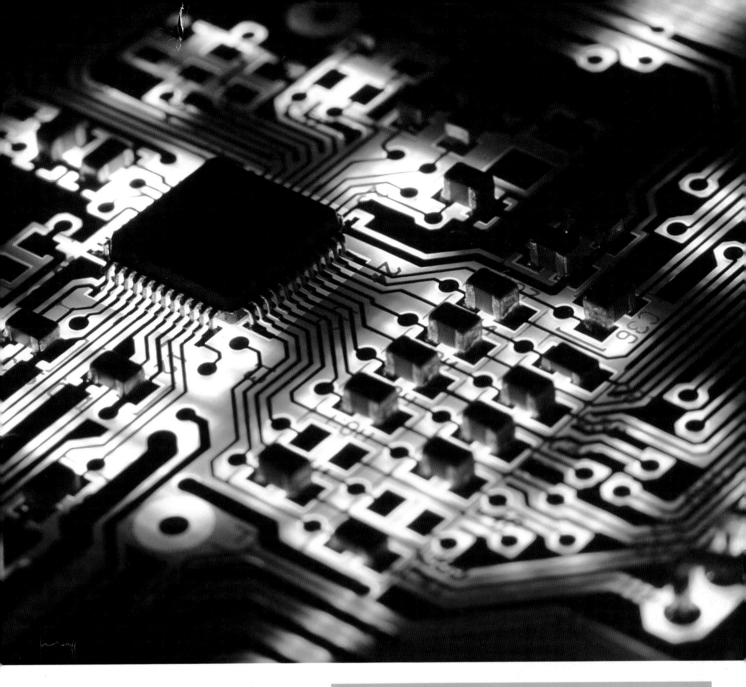

▲ The dark square above is a microchip. It is surrounded by a complex circuit of connections that pass information between the microchip and other parts of the machine.

Computers need **programs** to work. Programs are sets of instructions to run particular tasks. A math program can be quite simple, but a program that allows a robot to recognize a face is much more complex, and requires more processing power. As the processing power of microchips increases, robots will be able to tackle even more complex, demanding jobs.

ROBOFACTS: MOORE'S LAW

Moore's Law is named after Gordon Moore of the Intel computer company.

In 1965, Moore observed that technical advances could double the processing power of microchips about every two years.

Microchip processors have roughly followed Moore's Law over the years, allowing each new computer to be more powerful than the last model. Microchips are used in a robot's computer brain, so new robotic devices are also improving.

An Intel computer chip, compared with an American dime

ROBOT SENSES

Robots use devices, called sensors, to collect information about their environment. Sensors send this information to the robots' brains.

◄ This robot hand moves and grips much like a human one. A microchip controls its movements.

▼ The Dexter robot was built to handle objects safely. It can learn new actions to work on its own, or be operated at a distance by a human controller.

Robot sensors detect information in several ways. Video cameras allow robots to "see," while sound sensors, such as microphones, allow robots to "hear." To touch objects, **contact switches** and **strain gauges** help robots determine the amount of pressure needed to handle objects. This ensures that a robot applies an appropriate amount of pressure for grasping and picking up objects of different weights and sizes, such as a rubber balloon or a heavy crate.

Sensors are linked to the robot's computer brain by wires and cables. **Radio waves** or light beams can also be used to send information when there is some distance between the sensor and the computer.

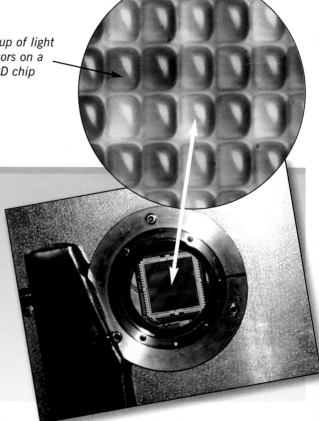

Close-up of light sensors on a CCD chip

ROBOFACTS: SECRETS OF SIGHT

Robots see by using a tiny light sensor, called a charge-coupled device, or CCD, which was invented in 1969 by Willard Boyle and George Smith from the United States. A CCD sensor has a small computer chip, covered with millions of linked, or coupled, capacitors.

When light falls on one of these capacitors, a tiny electric charge is generated. The computer chip detects the various light levels falling across the sensor, and converts this information into a visual image.

CCDs are not only used as robots' eyes. They are also used in digital photography.

◄ A scientist holds a six-legged robot "insect" called Genghis. Light sensors on the robot's head send visual information to goggles, letting the scientist see what Genghis sees.

▼ Genghis is one of several small robots that have been built to carry out simple tasks. Future robots based on this design could check and make repairs to machinery in hard-to-reach places.

SCHOOL FOR ROBOTS

Robots can be given simple sets of instructions for many jobs. For complex tasks, robots need to learn about their environment before they can respond to it.

▲ From 1966 to 1972, this robot, called Shakey, was used to pioneer robotic learning methods.

Making a computer version of the human brain has proven more difficult than early robot researchers had thought. Our brains have about 100 billion **brain cells**, which work together in ways that are just beginning to be understood. One of the brain's best abilities is that it can quickly sort a massive amount of information. For example, it can take in a complex scene at a glance, such as a landscape, and instantly focus on one part of it, such as a tiny bird.

▶ Centibots were made to work as a team, to search for objects in a target area. Each Centibot is not very smart, but they are efficient when they work together.

Computers can try to match our ability to sort information quickly, but the processing power of microchips is only beginning to approach the ultra-fast calculating speeds needed for this.

ROBOFACTS: YO-YO ROBOT

A yo-yo robot arm, developed by a team at the Jozef Stefan Institute of Slovenia, is helping to research which tasks a robot might do instead of humans.

The arm was linked to a video camera and had sensors that gave it some feel for the up-and-down motion of a toy yo-yo.

The arm's robotics engineer Leon Îlajpah believes that future versions of the yo-yo arm could be used in homes for many daily jobs. Some day, the yo-yo arm could perform such tasks as cleaning up, painting, preparing drinks, and even chopping firewood for burning.

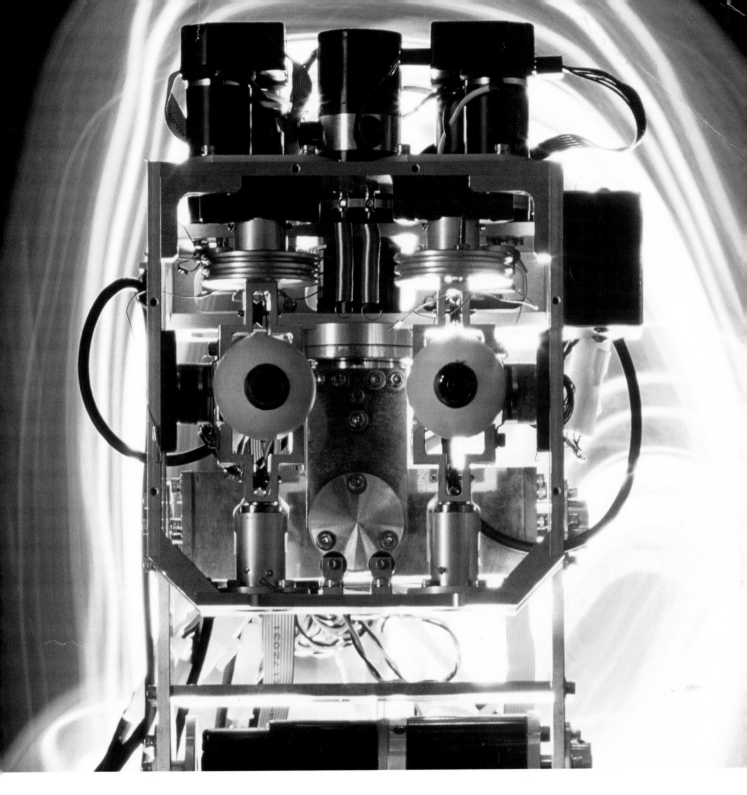

Rather than trying to develop one super-powerful robot, an American research group developed the Centibots, up to 100 small robots that work together to learn about a new environment. Centibots can explore a strange area, map it, then search it. To do this, the Centibots send details to each other by radio as they criss-cross the ground, to make a shared computer map of the target zone. When the map is complete, they switch into search mode. Future versions of the Centibots could be used to find survivors after earthquakes, hurricanes, or other disasters.

▲ Here is the face of Wabian, an experimental robot with two legs, arms, hands, and eyes. Wabian is the opposite of the Centibots because it is a single machine with a powerful computer running its systems. It can walk and can recognize and respond to several human gestures, including "come here" and "go away."

ROBOTS THAT "THINK"

▲ They may look real, but these "robots" have actors inside.

Robots with artificial intelligence are found only in books and movies today, but scientists are working to develop them.

Elmer and Elsie were two early robots with limited artificial intelligence, which allowed them to perform simple tasks without the help of humans. They were built by American scientist William Grey Walter in 1948. These three-wheeled robots were called tortoises because of their oval outer casings.

In the 1990s, Australian scientist Rodney Brooks developed Cog, a robot built with a head, torso, and arms. The idea was that if a robot received information from its **sensors** like a human, then it might start to learn about its environment the way we do.

A light track marks this tortoise's movements

▲ Elmer and Elsie were programmed to roll over to an outlet to recharge their batteries when they ran low.

◄ Cog does not have legs, but its body, arms, and hands move like those of a human. It has video cameras for eyes, and microphones for ears.

Electric motors in each hand give fingers and thumbs full motion

Qrio weighs 15.4 pounds (7 kg). Qrio is very quiet when it is working

► The name Qrio stands for Quest for cuRIOsity. Qrio robots are 23 inches (58 centimeters) tall. Qrio can walk and dance, and push itself upright if it is knocked over.

Qrio is a type of advanced robot that can recognize faces and voices, from information received from a built-in camera and two microphones. These robots can also do some unusual things, such as disco dancing! Despite these impressive skills, Qrio is some way from having artificial intelligence.

ROBOFACTS:
QRIO AT SCHOOL

In 2005, a Qrio robot went to a school in San Diego, California. The purpose was for researchers to study how toddlers might behave with a non-human companion.

The results were fascinating. According to researcher Fumihide Tanaka, the toddlers were not confused by having a robot in their midst, but it took a while for them to get used to it. The children treated Qrio with more care than they would treat a regular toy. For example, they helped the little robot back to its feet when it fell over. The children also enjoyed having Qrio's company when it joined their dance classes.

Later, another robot named Rubi joined the class. Rubi had a TV screen on its chest that displayed information to children. Rubi became a teaching assistant in the classroom.

Movements are controlled mostly by a nearby computer, using a radio link

Qrio can climb slopes with an incline of up to 10 degrees

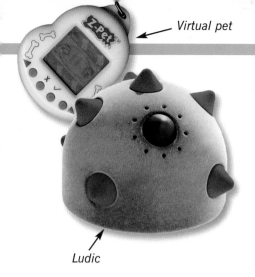

Virtual pet

Ludic

▲ The Z-Pet was a "virtual pet" made in Japan. In 1996, the Dutch Philips company came out with Ludic, an "electronic friend" that responded to touch as well as voice commands.

ROBOTOYS

Many toy makers manufacture top-selling gadgets that are hard to produce. In recent years, robots have been near the top of many children's wish lists at Christmas time.

Toy robots powered by wind-up spring mechanisms or batteries have been popular since the 1950s. Robotoys with serious computing power arrived only in the 1990s, when virtual pets became popular. These pocket-sized gadgets combined a digital clock with a range of on-screen functions that included eating, sleeping, and even going to the bathroom!

Robots in the home took a step forward in 1999, with the first robotic animals. The Sony company's robodogs were among the most advanced. Each one had a "personality" that included such things as barking a greeting and wagging its tail.

Computer experts could also program their robodogs to do new things, such as dancing or other body movements.

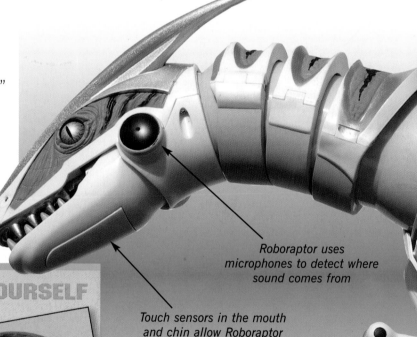

Roboraptor uses microphones to detect where sound comes from

Touch sensors in the mouth and chin allow Roboraptor to gently bite

ROBOFACTS: BUILD IT YOURSELF

Most robot research is carried out by teams working in high-tech laboratories. However, anyone can make a start in robotics by using inexpensive build-it-yourself kits.

The robot shown here is one of a series designed to show off simple features. About an hour of careful assembly results in a walking machine that marches along on circular feet at the clap of your hands. The secret lies in the sound sensor that sends a start signal to the robot's electric motor.

▲ The falling cost of computer chips makes it possible to create smart robotic toys cheaply. Roboraptor includes electronic features that would have once been used only in the best research laboratories.

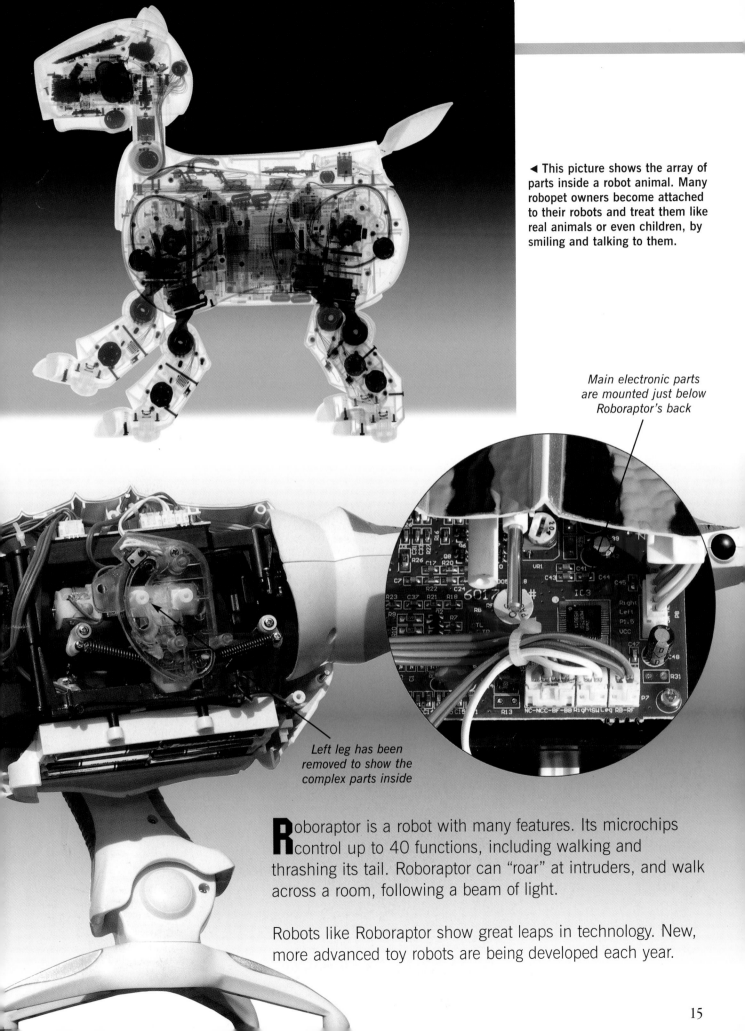

◀ This picture shows the array of parts inside a robot animal. Many robopet owners become attached to their robots and treat them like real animals or even children, by smiling and talking to them.

Main electronic parts are mounted just below Roboraptor's back

Left leg has been removed to show the complex parts inside

Roboraptor is a robot with many features. Its microchips control up to 40 functions, including walking and thrashing its tail. Roboraptor can "roar" at intruders, and walk across a room, following a beam of light.

Robots like Roboraptor show great leaps in technology. New, more advanced toy robots are being developed each year.

ROBOT HIGHWAYS

Automated computer systems are already built into many vehicles. One day, there might be robotic vehicles that are programmed to operate on their own.

Like many daily tasks, driving is more complicated than it seems. Autopilots that take command during flight have been standard on aircraft for many years. However, the sky is simpler to navigate in than busy highways and streets, where there are more obstacles, including other vehicles, pedestrians, and stray dogs.

▲ This robotic SUV was a race winner in 2005. It steered with information received from a tracking system on the roof.

▲ A 1950s idea of how a robot driver might look.

▲ Vehicle computers will communicate with sensors and each other to stay on course. For example, small radio beacons at road junctions communicate with in-car receivers. These then order the vehicle computer to prepare its systems for a possible turn.

In 2005, a race between robot cars took place across the Mojave Desert in the United States. The winning robocar used computers, **laser** beams, and video cameras to navigate the 132-mile (212-kilometer) race. These devices have not been introduced to regular road vehicles yet, because there is a big difference between a desert trail and a busy highway. Adding robotic systems to cars, and adding sensors to roads and signposts is a next step in creating fully robotic vehicles.

1

Robotic vehicles are being developed one step at a time. Today, cars are available that have driving aids such as automatic braking, cruise control, rain-sensing windshield wipers, and lights that turn themselves on and off.

Automatic steering is already being tested in research vehicles. The feature uses cameras to send images of road markings to a computer. This adjusts the steering to keep vehicles from veering off the highway.

ROBOFACTS: ROBOT BRAKES

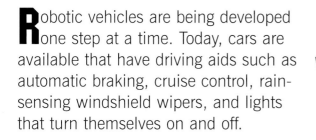

Robotic systems to keep vehicles on the road a safe distance apart are available.
1 The car behind (blue) sends a beam of radio waves toward the car in front (red).
2 If the front car slows down, the blue car's computer will sense it and signal the car to apply the brakes.

Design for a future robocar from Lexus

Area swept by radio beam

White circles mark some computerized systems aboard this car:
1 Sensor checks for traffic ahead and applies brakes if needed.
2 Active system keeps car stable on corners.
3 Tire pressures, suspension, and engine are all checked and controlled by computer systems.
4 Many functions can be operated by controls built into the steering wheel, called a switching center.
5 Automatic electronic parking brake.
6 Rear tire pressure sensors check for leaks in the tires.
7 Rear suspension is adjusted to be firm or soft, according to speed and the type of road surface.

HELPFUL HUMANOIDS

Robots are now becoming useful for everyday life. Humanoids **are robots that are built in human form, and might eventually replace humans for many tasks.**

▲ The Papero personal robot can identify 650 phrases and speak 3,000 different words. It can recognize up to ten people by checking their facial patterns using its two video eyes. It can also work a TV and check emails.

Humanoids are examples of an important kind of robot being developed in Japan. The goal is to make a reliable robot that can be used to help look after people, including the elderly.

There are good reasons for developing robots that can take care of people. By 2025, about one-quarter of Japan's population will be elderly. Other countries also have aging populations. For example, about 72 million Americans are expected to be over 65 years old by the year 2030. Humanoid robots in homes, hospitals, and nursing homes could make life easier for health care professionals at these facilities.

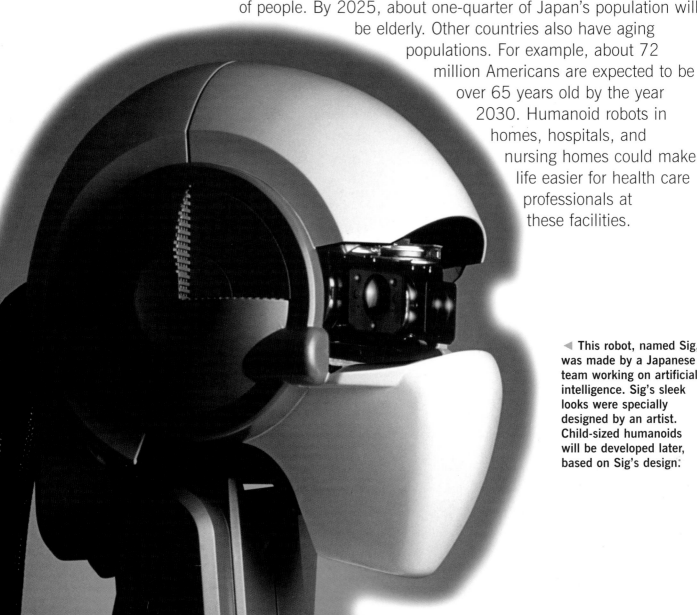

◀ This robot, named Sig, was made by a Japanese team working on artificial intelligence. Sig's sleek looks were specially designed by an artist. Child-sized humanoids will be developed later, based on Sig's design.

ROBOFACTS: FROM CLANKY TINBOT TO SLEEK METAL MAN

Researchers from the Honda company in Japan have worked on robots since the 1980s. The E0 model was a pair of legs that took nearly five seconds between steps.

The E1 improved on this timing. In 1993, Honda's engineers added a body and arms to make the P1. As well as being able to walk, P1 could open doors and pick up objects.

P2 could walk and also take stairs. It did not need trailing cables to control it. The sleek P3 performed best of all, and many of its parts were shrunk to fit a smaller and lighter form.

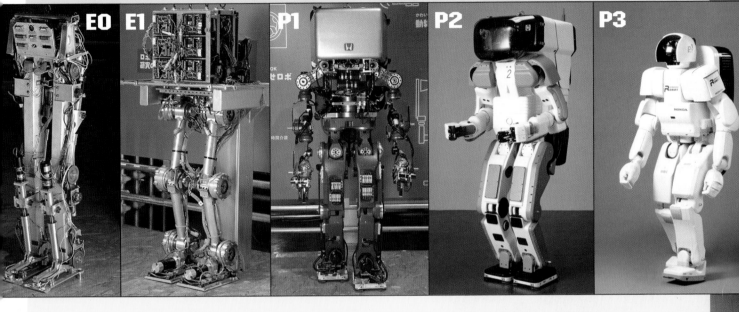

Most robots that have been developed to work with humans are small, so they can walk around in rooms and offices without getting in the way. Their appearance has also proved important, since people react better to robots that look friendly.

▲ ▶ The Asimo robot from Honda is an advanced machine that can walk, run, be a receptionist, and even carry drinks on a tray.

Powered
arm

Powered
leg

▲ HAL-5's arms and legs
are powered by batteries
held in a backpack.

HUMAN OR MACHINE?

Cybernetics **is the field of study that examines robotic control and communications in machines and living things.**

Cybernetics scientists have developed artificial mechanical limbs for people who have lost theirs in accidents. There has also been research into mechanical **exoskeletons**, which are very strong robotic bodies that people could wear over their clothing. The HAL-5 (Hybrid Assistive Limb), from Japan, could be worn to give people protection in dangerous places, such as battle zones.

One of the leaders in linking humans with machines is the British Professor Kevin Warwick, nicknamed "Captain **Cyborg**." In 1998, Warwick was the first person to have a microchip inserted into his arm. Using the microchip as a built-in radio controller, Warwick could switch lights on and off, and make electric doors open and shut from a distance, by sending a signal from the chip.

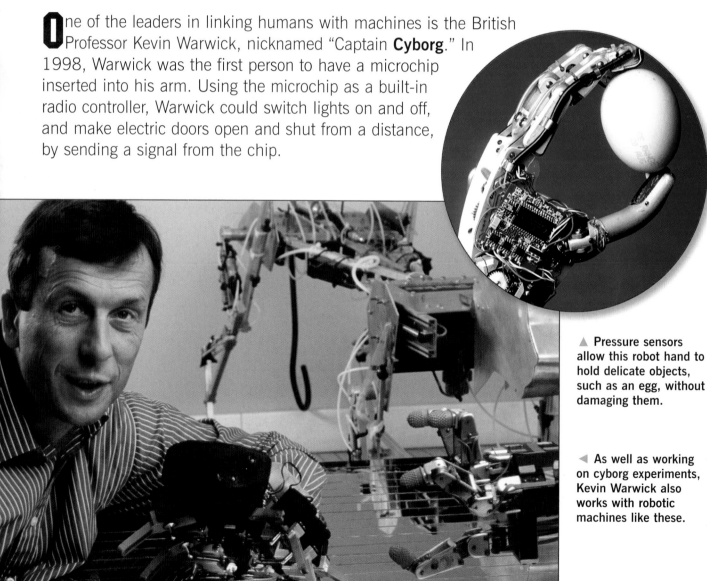

▲ Pressure sensors allow this robot hand to hold delicate objects, such as an egg, without damaging them.

◀ As well as working on cyborg experiments, Kevin Warwick also works with robotic machines like these.

ROBOFACTS:
A NEW AGE OF LIVING ROBOTICS?

Various experiments have aimed at linking computers with animal or human brains. In the 1990s, researchers at the Max Plancke Institute in Germany showed that it is possible to join living nerves to microchips.

A single brain cell was taken from a rat and carefully attached to a microchip. When the cell was connected to the chip, electrical signals were passed back and forth between them.

Researchers think it may be possible to repeat this with human brain cells. Ideas include a link between the brain and a video camera to make an electronic eye for the blind. A link to a microphone could also help the deaf. Researchers also think that eventually it may be possible to download daily experiences to a computer disk, to help people who suffer from memory loss.

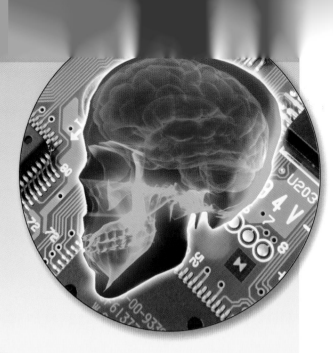

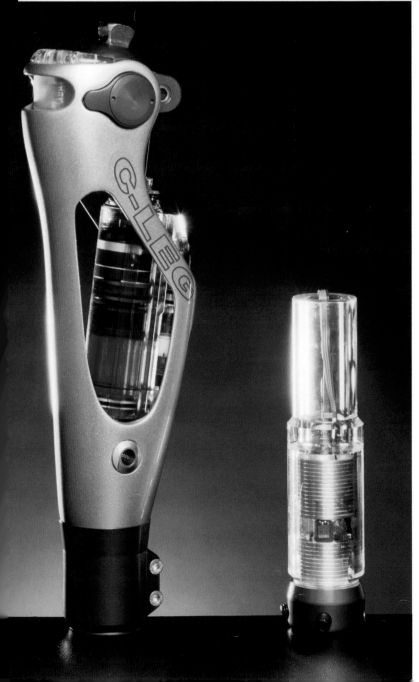

▲ The electric-motor gripper weighs just 19 ounces (539 grams). Its rubber coating helps hold things.

◀ The C-Leg's tiny computer checks and adjusts movement 50 times a second, for a smooth stride. The C-Leg can even go up hills and slopes.

Robotic developments have resulted in some amazing machines, but some simpler robotic devices continue to help people. The C-Leg, made by the Otto Bock company of Germany, can replace an amputated leg. The C-leg has a microchip that controls a piston, which pumps up and down to provide walking action. The battery-powered C-Leg can change from walking to climbing mode, just by tapping the toe.

ROBOTS vs HUMANS

Robots cannot think creatively, like humans, but they can process difficult calculations in seconds.

Computers first beat humans at chess in 1997, when the IBM Deep Blue **supercomputer** defeated one of the world's best chess players, American Gary Kasparov. Some people thought Deep Blue was thinking about the game, but it was simply using a sophisticated chess program.

Deep Blue won because it could process information quickly. It could calculate the outcome of about 200 million possible moves in a single second. Kasparov analyzed only three or four moves in the same amount of time, but he used skill and experience to win some of the games in the chess match.

▲ The epic chess match between Kasparov and Deep Blue was the subject of this book.

May 11th, 1997
Computer won world champion of chess
(Deep Blue)   (Garry Kasparov)

(Reuters = Kyodo News)

▲ Deep Blue's victory was captured by TV cameras for all the world to see.

▼ This chess board is truly robotic. A small robot rolls back and forth to move the pieces during a match.

Sleek casings cover Blue Gene's working parts

The IBM Blue Gene supercomputer is even faster than Deep Blue. Blue Gene can run more than 280 trillion calculations per second. In the near future, experts believe the speed can be further increased, perhaps to more than 367 trillion calculations per second.

▲ Many chess programs can be used on home computers. Even a simple program can provide you with a tough challenge.

Human and robot shown to scale with Blue Gene computer

▲ This is the IBM Blue Gene supercomputer. It is much faster than Deep Blue, shown in the picture at top right.

Supercomputers like Blue Gene lead the way in computer processing speed, and are important for robotics. Many of the lessons learned in developing these advanced machines can be applied to making the microchips used by robots. A faster microchip brain allows a robot to perform complex tasks more efficiently, especially those needing the most processing power.

ROBOFACTS: RACING IN THE DESERT

In 2005, robots replaced jockeys in a camel race in the Persian Gulf state of Abu Dhabi.

In the race, ten robot jockeys each took charge of a camel, and they galloped off across the sand.

Human operators ran behind them, holding portable radio-control units.

Robots were introduced to camel racing after it became illegal to use jockeys under the age of 18.

ROBOTS IN CHARGE

The power and speed of computers make them useful in everyday life. From banks to transportation, robots help run the world.

▲ This elevated train is completely automated, with systems that open and shut the doors, start the train, and apply the brakes at the end of a trip.

Robotic systems make things run more smoothly in our busy world. For example, many cities and airports have automatic trains that transport people quickly and safely. Roads are becoming automated to control traffic and reduce congestion.

◄ Jetliners all come with robotic control systems to simplify the work of the human crews.

► Here are some automated systems used around the world.
1 Scanners can check retina patterns in the eye to confirm a person's identity.
2 Robots are used in many factories to assemble goods.
3 Automatic bank machines distribute money when needed.
4 In big cities, highway and traffic lights are increasingly computer-controlled.
5 The Internet links machines and humans across the world.
6, 7, 8 Automated video systems hunt for criminal activity. Robodogs, like this experimental model, may soon join them.

The world's money supplies are run almost completely by robotic systems, mostly with great efficiency and speed. However, computerization introduces a few problems. Some people prefer human contact over robots. The use of security cameras in banks also makes people worry about their privacy.

ROBOFACTS: 80 YEARS OF SCI-FI KILLER ROBOTS

It is not surprising that many people have mixed feelings about robots, since evil robots have starred in many science fiction books and movies.

One of the earliest "badbots" was Maria, an elegantly designed robot that starred in the 1927 German movie, *Metropolis*. In this film, the robot was built to stir up trouble among human workers of a futuristic city.

A robot built to look like a female is called a gynoid

Deadly robots featured in many magazines of the 1930s and 1940s

2

3

7

5

8

4

6

These tough-looking robots are typical of those shown in modern comic books

THE RED MAGICIAN: By John Russell Fearn
1/-

FANTASY
THRILLING SCIENCE FICTION

Amazing Scientific Romance
MENACE OF THE METAL-MEN
And Other Great Imaginative Adventures
by
JOHN REYNOLDS & L.E GURDON
ERIC F. RUSSELL, LELE EATON
and others.

FUTURE
NOV SCIENCE FICTION
25¢

TATUM!
SHECKLEY
ALL STORIES NEW

CHOPPERCHICK COMICS
KILLER ROBOTS
WILL SMASH THE WORLD!
CYBER TURBO 5000
ALPHA X DELUXE

MEDIA

The theme of dangerous robots continues to be a science fiction theme

25

THINGS TO COME?

Robotic science is moving fast, and it is certain that future robots will be capable of even more than those of today.

Advances are happening in all areas of robotics. Microchip processing speeds keep improving, chips are shrinking in size, and they are becoming cheaper to make. This means more processing capacity can be packed aboard new robots.

▲ Seen here in a microscope picture, a human hair looks huge and scaly. The carbon nano circuit (arrowed) is shown on the same scale. It does the same job as a silicon chip, but the small size helps to give it more speed.

In 2006, scientists developed an even smaller microchip. The **nano circuit** was five times thinner than the width of a human hair. Instead of being laid on silicon, the nano circuit was assembled on a tiny tube of **carbon**.

When nano circuits are perfected, these ultra-tiny chips will allow even faster processing, bringing the dream of artificial intelligence another step closer.

ROBOFACTS: WILL ROBOTS RULE US ALL?

The world is already run with the help of powerful computers, but the A.I. robot brain of science fiction has yet to be developed.

Could ultra-smart A.I. machines be a danger to the world as we know it? Would intelligent robots want to get rid of humans and take over the world? We do not yet know.

The 1968 space movie *2001: A Space Odyssey* showed what could happen if a robotic system really did decide to have things its own way.

In the movie, a spaceship's robot brain, HAL 9000, starts killing the crew. Just one of the astronauts manages to survive HAL's deadly actions, which were caused by problems with its computer software **program**.

The surviving astronaut managed to switch off HAL before it killed him, too

One of HAL 9000's spy cameras

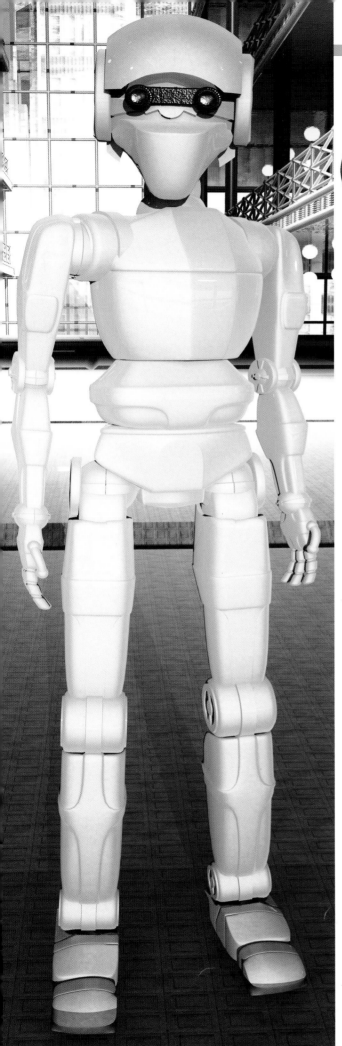

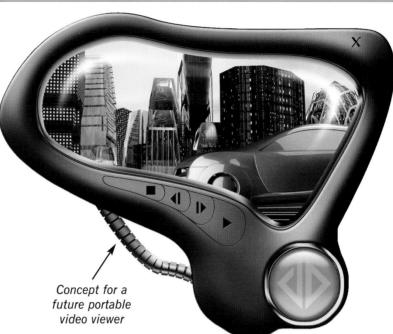

X

Concept for a future portable video viewer

◀ **A robot goes about its work in an imaginary futuristic city. One research company has suggested covering these robots with soft material, in case of collision with humans.**

▲ **A robocar glides through the streets of this possible future world. Traffic is controlled by central computers, using information from millions of sensors laid across the city.**

What will life be like in a future robot world? Carnegie Mellon University in Pittsburgh, Pennsylvania is planning a research center, called Robot City, to examine some of the possibilities. The university will use the space to build and test robots for maintenance work such as planting grass, mowing lawns, cleaning and maintaining security.

Robot City research is important, but it is impossible to say what a future robotic city will be like. We can predict some things. For example, computers will control many city systems in the future, such as heating, cooling, cleaning, and regulating water supplies. Millions of sensors in roads, walkways, and buildings will update the city's robot brains, giving information updates on what is happening in the city, and where events occur.

▲ A sketch of robots from the play *Rossum's Universal Robots*, **or** *RUR*, **from a London theatre production in 1923.**

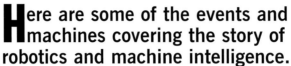

TIME TRACK

Here are some of the events and machines covering the story of robotics and machine intelligence.

▲ HAL 9000 was in charge of this spaceship in the movie *2001: A Space Odyssey*.

2500 B.C.   Greek myth of Talos, a metal giant built to guard the island of Crete.

1642   French mathematician Blaise Pascal makes a calculator.

1823   English mathematician Charles Babbage designs the Difference Engine, an ancestor of the programmable computer.

1893   American inventor George Moore builds a robot man, powered by steam. It can walk at up to nine miles per hour (14.5 kilometers per hour).

1920   Czech writer Karel Capek writes a stage play about robots trying to take over from humans. The word "robot" was coined by Capek's brother, from the Czech word "robota," meaning "work."

1927   German director Fritz Lang makes the movie *Metropolis*, starring a female humanoid robot.

1943   The first electronic computer, Electronic Numerical Integrator And Computer (ENIAC), is built.

1948   William Grey Walter creates Elmer and Elsie, two robots known as tortoises. Elmer and Elsie can find their way to a charging point when their batteries run low.

1950   British mathematician Alan Turing devises the Turing Test. Turing's work has led many to call him the father of computer science.

1956   The term artificial intelligence (A.I.) is used for the first time. In 1959, a laboratory to study A.I. is started by researchers Marvin Minsky and John McCarthy.

1960   The term cyborg is created by Manfred E. Clynes and Nathan S. Kline, referring to their idea of a machine-enhanced human who could survive in dangerous environments.

1965   Gordon Moore proposes Moore's Law in an article published in *Electronics Magazine*.

1966   Shakey is the first mobile robot that can solve simple problems, such as shifting blocks or moving past obstacles. Shakey is used for A.I. experiments until 1972.

▲ The microchip makes calculations in computers and robotic devices.

1968 The first computer circuit on a chip of silicon is perfected. The "microchip" becomes the basis of all computing machines made ever since, including robots.

1968 The movie *2001: A Space Odyssey* is released. Directed by Stanley Kubrick, the movie stars the A.I. brain HAL 9000, which takes over the spaceship *Discovery* and kills all but one of its crew.

1969 The charge-coupled device (CCD) is invented by Willard Boyle and George Smith, working at the laboratories of AT&T Bell. CCDs are now the standard light sensor used in digital cameras, for taking both still pictures and video.

1971 Computers start to come into general use. They are followed by desktop models in the 1980s. In many countries today, they are in every office and most homes.

1986 Honda starts developing a line of experimental robots, each one a little more advanced than the previous model. By 2005, the Honda Asimo can walk, talk, climb stairs, and deliver drinks.

1997 Machines beat humans at chess for the first time, when the IBM Deep Blue supercomputer beats human chess champion Gary Kasparov, in a six-game match.

1998 British Professor Kevin Warwick has a radio transmitter inserted into his arm. Using it, he can control nearby doors, lights, and computer devices.

1999 The first robotic dogs become available from Sony.

2004 The humanoid Robosapien goes on sale in toy stores. It is later joined by other advanced machines, including the dinosaur-like Roboraptor.

2005 A robotic vehicle finishes a desert course to win a long-distance robocar rally.

2006 The first experimental nano circuit chip shrinks the size of microchips even further. Developed versions will run much faster than present-day silicon microchips.

2010-2015 New homes and vehicles may be fitted with simple A.I. systems. In homes, A.I. systems may run domestic services and security. Vehicles may drive themselves on special sensor-equipped highways.

▲ Robosapien has up to 67 functions, including throwing, kicking, walking, and dancing.

▼ The Pleo robopet of 2006 has sight, sound, and touch. It can explore its environment, much like a real animal. Pleo's maker, Ugobe, hopes that it will be as successful as other robot pets.

Pleo is modelled after the appearance of a one-week old baby Camarasaurus dinosaur

► The CCD light-sensing chip forms the basis of robotic "eyes."

GLOSSARY

Artificial intelligence (A.I.) A term that describes machines that can accomplish tasks that require thought.

Brain cell One of the microscopic units that make up a brain. The human brain consists of about 100 billion cells.

Capacitor Device that can store an electric charge for a limited time.

Carbon Chemical that has two pure forms, diamond and graphite. Impure forms include soot, charcoal, and coal.

CCD Short for charge-coupled device (CCD). A CCD changes light into electricity. These signals are processed by the robot's chip and converted to visual information.

Circuit Any electronic linkage that joins two or more parts together.

Computer software Another name for a computer program, which is the set of instructions used by a computer. Hardware is the name for the machine, including wiring and other physical parts of a computer.

Contact switch An electronic device that gives a signal when things touch, such as a robotic hand coming into contact with an object.

Cybernetics The field of robotic control and communications.

Cyborg Name for a blend of living and machine systems. Cyborgs used to be found only in the pages of science fiction. Recent work has proved that linking machine electronics and living nerve tissue can work.

Digital The name for any device that uses the binary code. Binary code uses a series of ones and zeros to represent information.

Exhaust pipe A type of chimney used to carry waste gases away from an engine.

Exoskeleton A strong metal and plastic outer casing that can be worn to boost body strength.

Humanoid Having a form similar to that of a human. A humanoid robot has a head, arms, body, and legs in roughly the right places.

A gynoid is the name given to a robot designed to look like a female human.

Laser A device that projects an intense, pencil-thin beam of light.

Microchip The tiny part of any computer or robotic device that makes calculations. Microchips have circuit patterns on small pieces, or chips, of silicon.

Nano circuit Even smaller than a conventional silicon microchip, a carbon nano circuit is made at the "nano" scale, one nanometer (nm) being one billionth of a meter.

Program The set of instructions that are fed into a computer to make it work.

Radio waves Form of energy used to transmit sound, but can also be used to send and receive digital information.

Retina A layer at the back of the eye containing cells that are sensitive to light. They trigger nerve impulses that travel through the optic nerve to the brain, where a visual image is formed.

Sensor The term for any device that imitates the human senses of touch, taste, sight, smell, or hearing. Robotic sensors include cameras for seeing, and microphones for hearing.

Silicon Dark gray material used in making electronic circuits, including microchips. Silicon is a semiconductor, which is a material that can act as an on-off switch.

Steam engine An engine that uses the expansion of steam from boiling water to make power.

Strain gauge A sensor that can detect force, or strain, as well as contact. Strain gauges help robots to safely pick up delicate objects.

Supercomputer A powerful computer with high processing speed.

Suspension Springs and other shock-absorbing parts.

They are designed to give a vehicle a smooth ride, while moving over a rough surface.

Transistor A device that is used to control or direct electricity.

Turing test A test for artificial intelligence, named after Alan Turing, who devised it in 1950.

Vacuum tube A type of delicate glass-and-metal electronic part that was widely used before transistors and microchips.

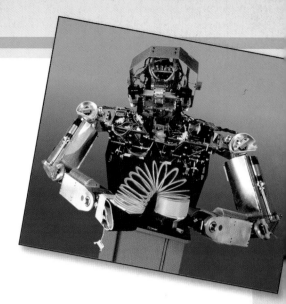

▲ Robots like this are built to find out about their environment. One day, such experiments may lead to truly intelligent machines.

This walking robot uses a light beam to spot and avoid objects in its path

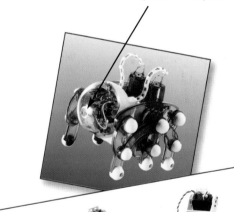

ROBOZONES: NEXT STEPS

Robots are fascinating machines, and a great way to find out how they work is to build one from the many kits that are available.

The German Fischertechnik company offers computer and robotic kits, as does Lego, the company best known for its toy construction bricks.

Ready-built robots are also available for purchase, such as Roboraptor, and the humanoid Robosapien, as well as the more recent Robosapien V2. Sony does not make robopets anymore, but some are available for purchase from the Internet.

Many of these ready-built robots offer the chance to program new functions. The Internet is a good place for keeping up with robotic news, and you can visit communities of robot enthusiasts online.

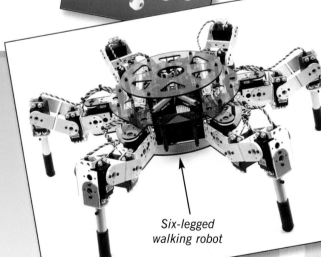

Six-legged walking robot

INDEX

Acknowledgements
We wish to thank all those individuals and organizations that have helped to create this publication. Information and images were supplied by:
ActivMedia Robotics, Alpha Archive, BMW, Boeing Corp, Carnegie Mellon University, Cyberdyne Inc, DARPA, Carl Goodman, Gusto, Fujitsu Corp, Hitachi Corp, Honda Motor Corp, IBM, IS Robotics, Intel Corp, iStockphoto, David Jefferis, Lexus, Peter Menzel, MIT CSAIL Humanoid Robotics Lab, Lynxmotion Inc, Andreas Maryanto, MIT AI Lab, NEC Corp, Nissan Corp, Otto Bock, Gavin Page/Design Shop, Philips Electronics, Rakbi Centre, Robotics Centre of Qatar, Science Photo Library, Sony Corp, SRI International, Stanford University, Ugobe Inc, University of Massachusetts, University of Washington, VAG, WowWee Ltd